CRAFTS FROM WORLD CULTURES

Easy-to-Make
Multicultural Art Activities

by Janice Veith and Anne Weber
illustrated by Susan Pinkerton

Dedicated to:
Marie Veith — thank you for being an unwavering source of love and
inspiration for your family. JV

My husband, Mitch Weber, for his encouragement, support, and, most of all,
his love. To my mother, Mary Emerson, for her tender touch
and unconditional love. AW

Publisher: Roberta Suid
Design, Production, & Typesetting: Susan Pinkerton
Copy Editor: Carol Whiteley
Editor: Annalisa Suid

Other Monday Morning multicultural materials:
Storybooks Teach About World Cultures (MM 1998) by Tanya Lieberman,
and *Patterns for World Cultures* (MM 1997) by Marilynn G. Barr

APR - - 1997

ACKNOWLEDGEMENTS

The authors would like to thank these special people for their valuable time and assistance:

Burbank Library Reference Desk staff
Joan Benedetti, Craft and Folk Art Museum
Mauriora Kingi, N.Z. Maori Arts and Crafts Institute
Frazier Park School Teachers: Linda Curtis, Joanne Thunberg, Lois Lee, and Pete Liebl
Bobbe Fernandez, American Indian Council
Kyoko Kitsu Emerson
Larry Emerson
Marion Emerson
Yolanda Dixon
Cathy Tabor
Lynne Kennedy
Tamara Welch
Karen Thomas
Dr. Larry Keeter
Rosie Huning
Dawn Dobie
Buzz Kind
Dr. Farnaz Zandkarimi
Jossie Constantino
Jody Matthews
David Simon
Bob Tullmann
Susan Bates
Karen Kirk

We would also like to thank these extraordinary kids for making many of the crafts with us:

Neil Weber
Alyssa Veith
Nicholas Veith
Ellen Dobie
Heidi Tullmann
Kesha Huning
Patty Arrigo
Jason Garcia

CONTENTS

North and South America

Our world's rich heritage comes to life in the hands of children when they create crafts from other cultures. They can be tribal dancers wearing ceremonial masks, or painters in Mexico splashing color onto festive bowls, or ancient Egyptians creating hieroglyphics.

By exploring the traditions of many people, children can embark on an adventure around the globe and back in time. Children can envision the sights and sounds of faraway places: the drone of the didjeridoo and the sand deserts of the Australian aborigines or the brilliant night sky over the noisy streets of India during the Festival of Lights.

Through craft-making, children are also able to imagine what the world was like long ago. Most of our early ancestors had no written language. Knowledge was passed on to children by their parents and grandparents. Children today can understand the struggles of their ancestors and see the unwritten stories in the beauty of their great-grandmother's quilts.

Through this simple (but very exciting) way of exploring other cultures, you will be able to delight children and arouse their interest in learning. As you lead your children through the activities in this book, you will open a door to the world around them. You can help the children find the origins of the craft cultures by rotating a globe and searching a map.

How to Use This Book

Crafts from World Cultures has been divided into three sections: North and South America, Asia and Australia, and Africa and Europe. All of the instructions for all of the crafts are described in easy steps with accompanying pictures. At the bottom of each page is a brief paragraph about the particular craft's cultural background. Read this to your class, or let children read it to themselves. Certain crafts are accompanied by pattern pages.

As you venture into the world of multicultural crafts, please consider these ideas:

• Whenever possible, make the craft project yourself before teaching it to your class. Then, make the craft again along with the children. This will help you to guide them through the experience in the way the craft was originally taught to children by parents and grandparents for many generations. Encourage older children to pass the ideas on to younger children to keep the tradition going.

• Let the craft experience lead you and your children outside of the classroom. Visit the library, a museum, a senior citizen center, a festival, or a dance production.

• Feel free to make any changes in the projects that you feel will help the children be more successful and gain more from the experience. Some projects may need to be made more complex while others may need to be simplified to work best for the developmental level of your children.

• Be open to a rich and exciting exchange of ideas and discoveries. Often, children have valuable ideas or traditions to share that they have not had the opportunity to bring to school before.

• Collect and display authentic folk art and crafts whenever possible. It is especially educating if you also provide photographs of people from different cultures in their homes or at their jobs. Enrich craft experiences by supplementing the projects with food, music, pictures, maps, and globes.

• Explore and share your own traditions with your students. Invite others from your community to join the class.

• Make the time with your students an interactive experience.

ANDINKERA CLOTH

Materials:

sticky-back foam (insulation type)
wood block
ink pad
craft knife or scissors
cloth or paper

1. **Cut** shape from foam.

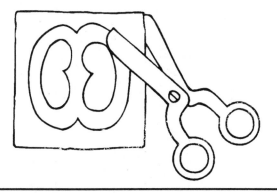

2. **Peel** off paper backing.

3. **Press** shape onto block.

4. **Print** on cloth or paper.

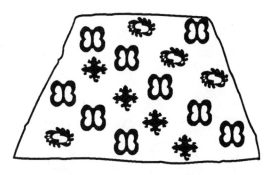

Andinkera was a king in **Africa** who wore robes covered with intricate designs. During a battle, King Andinkera was killed by the Ashanti, who took his robe as a trophy. Today, African clothing is often printed with Andinkera symbols. The colorful printed cloth is worn for many occasions by both men and women and is considered an elegant form of dress.

Materials:

bisque tile (unglazed)
grid paper cut to size of tile
pencil
ruler
markers
high-gloss coating spray

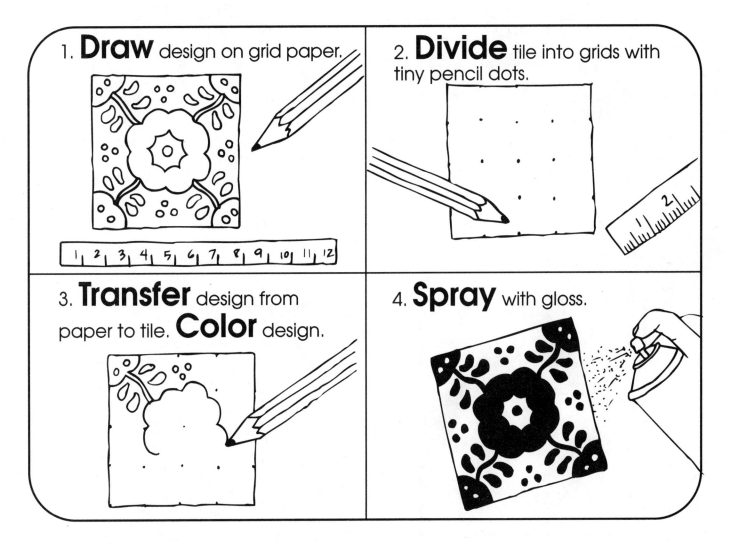

1. **Draw** design on grid paper.

2. **Divide** tile into grids with tiny pencil dots.

3. **Transfer** design from paper to tile. **Color** design.

4. **Spray** with gloss.

A monk traveling from Italy to **Spain** introduced the art of "free painting" on tiles at the beginning of the 16th century. This easy process was called "pisano" and was traditionally done in colors of yellow and blue with geometric designs. An azulejo (ah-zu-LEH-ho) is a Spanish-style colored tile. The Spanish built with tile rather than wood to keep their houses cooler.

Materials:

branch with several smaller branches or twigs
colored yarn strands
collected natural materials (long grasses, wild weed stocks, corn husks,
    seed pods, feathers, etc.)

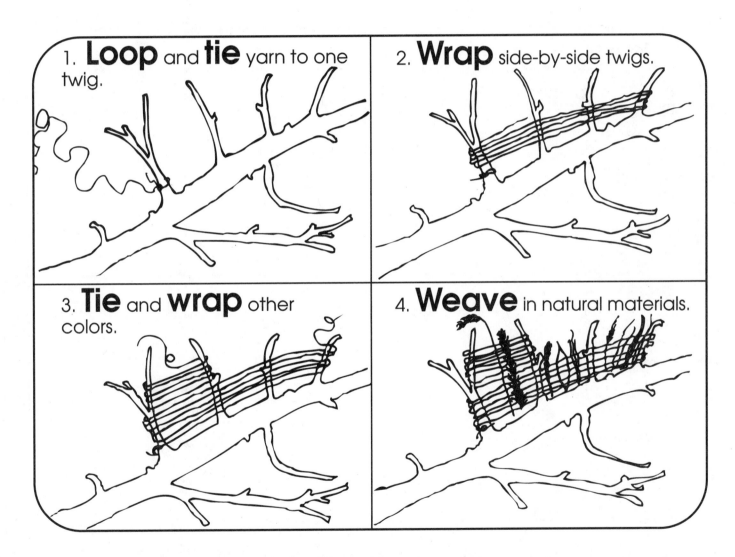

1. **Loop** and **tie** yarn to one twig.

2. **Wrap** side-by-side twigs.

3. **Tie** and **wrap** other colors.

4. **Weave** in natural materials.

Many cultures are known for their weaving, but **Greece** has some of the oldest tales relating to this skill. Ancient Greek myths tell of a weaving contest between a goddess and a boastful woman named Arachne. The goddess won, and turned poor Arachne into a spider. You may still see some of Arachne's relatives weaving webs to this day.

Materials:

self-hardening clay
toothpicks

1. **Shape** clay into button.

2. **Form** bump on back.

back view

3. **Pierce** bump with toothpick.

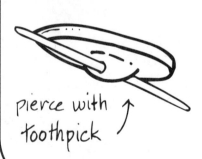

pierce with toothpick

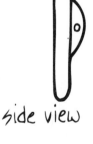

side view

4. **Press** designs in button with toothpick.

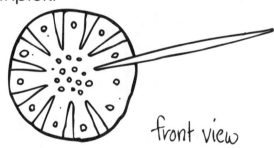

front view

Buttons from **ancient Egypt** are thought to be almost 4,000 years old. They were made from gold, bone, glass, and clay. Originally, buttons were worn only for decoration. Clothing was fastened with metal pins that looked like thin nails. The first working buttons were small discs that were pulled through holes in cloth fabric.

Materials:

self-hardening clay
paper bowl
black paint
paintbrush
spoon or carving tool

1. **Press** clay flat.

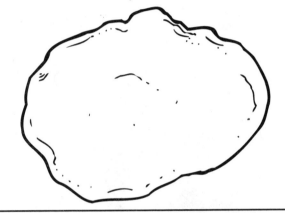

2. **Cover** bowl with clay. **Trim. Dry** about two hours.

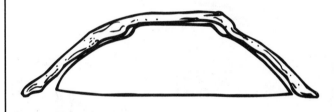

3. **Remove** bowl. **Paint** clay inside and out. Let **dry.**

4. **Carve** geometric designs with edge of spoon.

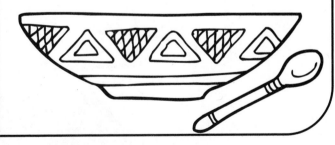

Skilled artists in **Africa** use sharp metal instruments to carve geometric designs in firm, sun-dried calabash gourds. Calabashes may be used for bowls, dishes, water jugs, musical instruments, or jewelry. The artists first use wood soot to blacken the calabashes. Then they carve decorative lines against the dark background.

CROWN OF LAUREL

Materials:

paper bag
leaves
scissors
stapler
tape

1. **Cut** headband from rim of paper bag.

2. **Collect** fresh leaves.

3. **Staple** leaves to band.

4. **Fit** headband. Tape ends to fit.

tape ends

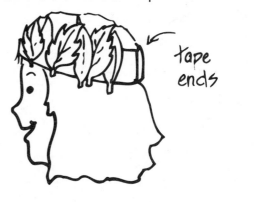

In the **Roman Empire**, crowns of laurel leaves were often worn by the emperors and generals. The leaves were tied in a circle to form a crown, which signified power and success. It's been said that Julius Caesar, a famous general of the Roman Empire, wore a crown of leaves to hide his lack of hair.

Materials:

small balloon (inflated and tied)
paper plate
colored paper (for mouth, hat, and tie)
yarn (for hair)
large feathers
scissors
glue

1. **Cut** holes for eyes and nose in plate.

small slits

2. **Cut** mouth, hat, and tie from paper.

3. **Glue** on paper pieces, hair, and feathers.

4. **Poke** tied end of balloon through slits for nose.

The "Great Gilles Carnival" in **Belgium** has been called the most unusual and festive parade in Europe. The procession weaves through the streets of Binche, Belgium, where gilles, or clowns, wear tall hats topped with ostrich plumes. The gilles dance for the cheering crowd. It is an honor in Belgium to be a gille in the carnival.

JIGSAW PUZZLE

Materials:

card stock
picture (drawn or cut from magazine or coloring book)
rubber cement
scissors
pencil

1. **Brush** rubber cement onto card stock.

2. **Press** on picture. **Smooth**. Let **dry**.

3. **Outline** puzzle pieces.

4. **Cut** out puzzle pieces.

In 1760, the first jigsaw puzzle was designed in **England** by John Spilsbury. Originally, maps were glued to sheets of thin wood, then cut into interlocking pieces. These puzzles were considered valuable as learning toys for children. Today, piecing together jigsaw puzzles is an enjoyable hobby for many people, young and old.

꧁꧂ JUMPING JACK ꧁꧂

Materials:

pre-cut pattern on card stock
hole punch
short paper fasteners
thin string
scissors
markers
glue

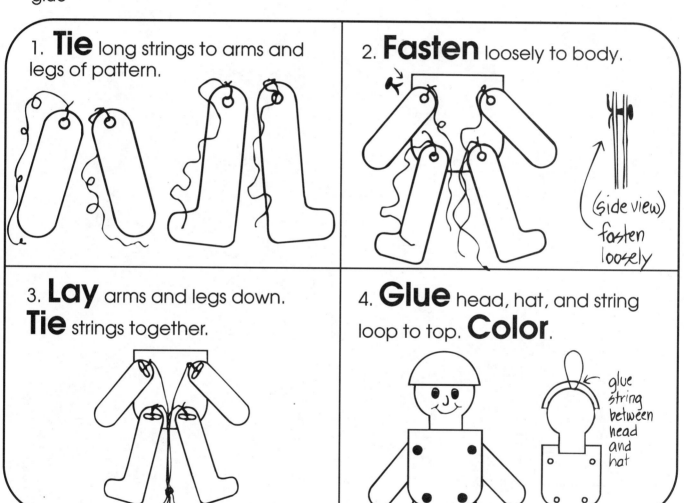

1. **Tie** long strings to arms and legs of pattern.

2. **Fasten** loosely to body.

(side view) fasten loosely

3. **Lay** arms and legs down. **Tie** strings together.

4. **Glue** head, hat, and string loop to top. **Color**.

glue string between head and hat

The woodcrafters of **Germany** were well known for their skill in making toys. These peasants spent long nights during the winter months carving toys from wood. When spring arrived, they traveled to cities to sell their toy figures. The Jumping Jack became the favorite wooden folk toy because children liked to pull the strings and make the little man jump.

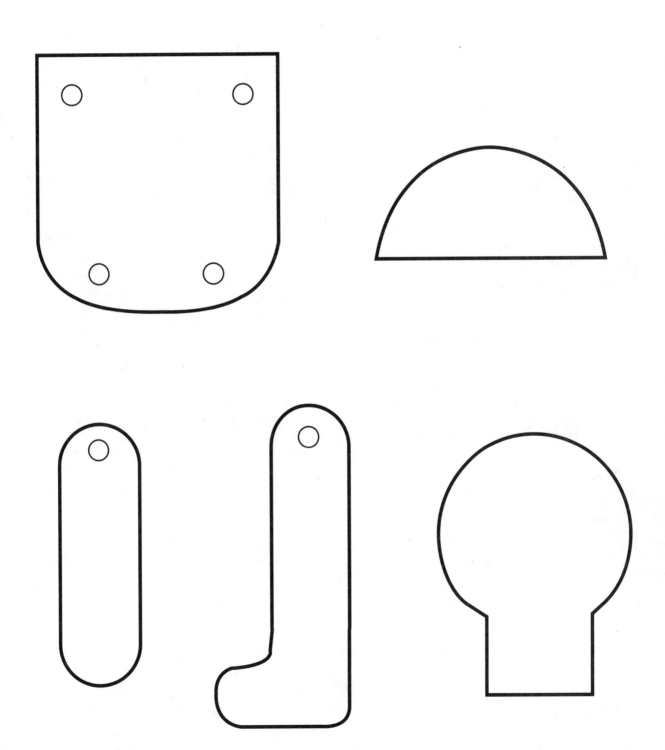

HIEROGLYPHICS

Materials:

gesso
paintbrush
used red brick
large nail
damp sponge
pencil

1. **Sponge** brick to clean.

2. **Brush** on gesso. Let **dry**.

3. **Draw** symbols with pencil.

4. **Carve** with nail.

When the Greeks first came to **ancient Egypt**, they called the Egyptian writing on tombs and temples "hieroglyphic"—"hiero" meaning "holy" and "glyph" meaning "writing." The hieroglyph symbols were written from right to left or from top to bottom. A child who learned to read and write hieroglyphs grew up to become a "scribe."

INDIGO PRINT

Materials:

white cotton fabric
blue fabric paint
shallow bowl
wood block
heavy string
potato (cut in half widthwise)
spoon

scissors
tape

1. **Wrap** wood block with string and **tie**.

2. **Carve** leaf shape into potato half with spoon.

3. **Dip** block and potato into paint.

4. **Print** pattern on fabric using potato and block.

Note: The block is used to create the lines. The potato creates the leaves.

The indigo plant, and the technique for making dye from it, were brought to **Africa** from India. African artists carved a shape into a dried calabash gourd and then printed patterns of the shape with indigo dye on white cotton. Designs of birds, fish, and leaves were sometimes combined with a lined pattern.

MARDI GRAS MASK

Materials:

paper plate
chopstick
markers
glitter
feathers
glue

masking tape
scissors

1. **Cut** paper plate and eye holes.

2. **Color**.

3. **Decorate**.

4. **Tape** stick to back of mask.

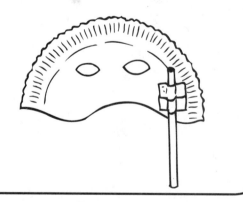

The Mardi Gras (MAR-dee grah) carnival originated in **France** in the 1880s. "Mardi Gras" is French for "Fat Tuesday." Today, people from many countries, including the United States, celebrate this wild and fun-filled event. In New Orleans, decorated floats carry the carnival king and his attendants, who throw trinkets to the crowd. Carnival goers wearing fancy costumes and masks dance to lively music.

MATROSHKA DOLLS

Materials:

two plastic eggs, one large, one small
one oblong bead (to fit into small egg)
white paint/white glue mixture (equal parts)
paintbrush
poster board bases for eggs
sandpaper (to roughen surface)

wax paper (to put under eggs while painting)
scissors
glue
markers
damp paper towel (to wipe sandpaper dust off of eggs)

1. **Sand** and **wipe** eggs.

sandpaper

wipe

2. **Brush** on mixture (two coats). **Dry**.

3. **Glue** bases on egg bottoms.

glue base

4. **Draw** and **color**. **Insert** bead in smaller egg.

Peasant families in **Russia** made matroshka "nesting" dolls for their children. The men carved the dolls from hollowed-out wood and the women painted the figures with brightly polished colors. At least two smaller dolls nestled within a large doll. The three dolls may have represented the grandmother, mother, and daughter in a family. The dolls were also painted as characters in fairy tales and used to help tell the stories to children.

Materials:

fresh flowers, with stems wrapped in wet paper towels in a plastic bag
1/2 paper plate
crayons or markers
ribbon
hole punch
stapler

1. **Color** back of plate half.

2. **Shape** into cone. **Staple**.

3. **Punch** holes on opposite sides.

punch holes

4. **Tie** on ribbon and **fill** with flowers.

There is a custom in **England** of secretly leaving a bouquet of flowers on a neighbor's doorstep on May 1st to welcome spring. This tradition may have begun in Egypt and Rome where festivals were held at the first sign of full-flowering plants and trees. In ancient Rome, Flora, the goddess of spring, was honored in a celebration called the "Festival of Flowers."

MOSAIC

Materials:

cardboard
pencil
cupcake pan filled with various seeds, beans, rice, and cereals
glue
clear sealant spray (optional)
brush

1. Sketch design on cardboard in pencil.

2. Spread glue over small sections at a time.

3. Fill in with materials.

4. Spray with sealant.

Mosaic, the art of using bits and pieces of materials to form a picture or pattern, may have been created in **Greece** in 400 B.C. Roman mosaics, displayed today in museums, were made of tiny glass cubes that reflected light. Other mosaics from ancient cultures capture scenes from everyday life or portray a mythological scene through marble and colorful stone.

Materials:

egg (allow egg to dry for two weeks before using)
markers (red for love, pink for success, blue for health, yellow for spirituality)
pencil
clear spray gloss

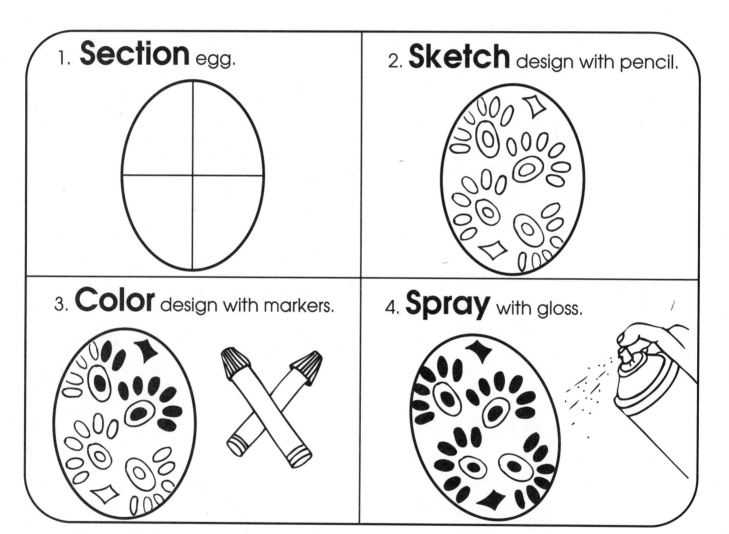

1. **Section** egg.

2. **Sketch** design with pencil.

3. **Color** design with markers.

4. **Spray** with gloss.

Psanky eggs, which are beautiful eggs with intricate and symbolic designs, are given as gifts by the people of the **Ukraine**. The Ukrainians brought the art of decorating eggs with them when they came to America in the 1860s.

SHAKARA RATTLE

Materials:

6 strings with beads tied to ends
rattle materials: pebbles, sand,
    beans, popcorn, seeds
sturdy paper cups
masking tape
thin dowel or unsharpened pencil

tissue paper pieces
paintbrushes
liquid starch
scissors
tempera paint in assorted colors

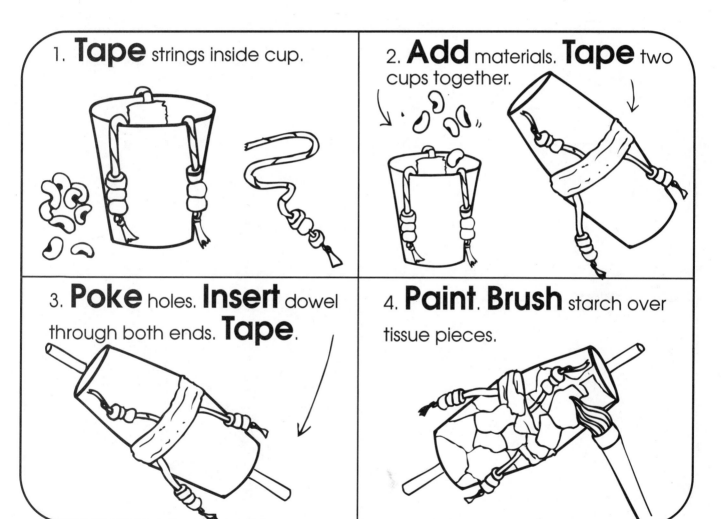

1. **Tape** strings inside cup.

2. **Add** materials. **Tape** two cups together.

3. **Poke** holes. **Insert** dowel through both ends. **Tape**.

4. **Paint**. **Brush** starch over tissue pieces.

Rattles were used as a "snake sound" in **ancient Egypt** to scare unwelcome visitors. Native Americans and Africans used rattles as musical instruments during ceremonies. Rattles were made from such materials as gourds, tortoise shells, horns, and clay. Crafters filled rattles with shells, beans, seeds, pebbles, and other bits of materials.

SHILLELAGH

Materials:

6 large sheets of newspaper
masking tape
green paint
paintbrush

1. **Roll** newspaper tightly. **Tape** closed.

roll and tape

2. **Bend** top of paper bundle over to form handle.

bend →

3. **Tape** around handle securely.

tape securely

4. **Paint** staff green.

green

A shillelagh (shill-LAY-lee) is a sturdy walking stick that was originally cut from the famous Shillelagh oak forest in **Ireland**. In American St. Patrick's Day parades, Irish people often carry a bright green shillelagh as a symbol of their homeland. It has been said that "The Irish heart is as stout as a shillelagh."

SPIRAL JEWELRY

Materials:

copper wire (10 gage or thinner)
  OR plastic-coated wire cut in 3 ft. lengths
empty soda can

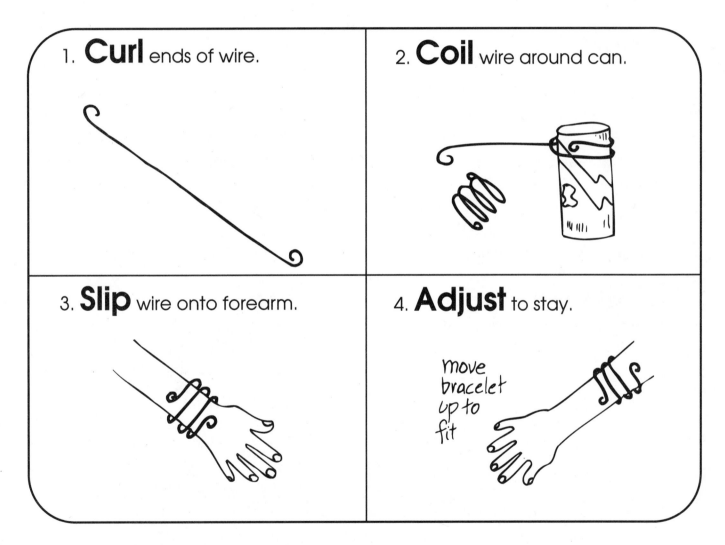

1. **Curl** ends of wire.

2. **Coil** wire around can.

3. **Slip** wire onto forearm.

4. **Adjust** to stay.

move bracelet up to fit

During the Bronze Age (around 2000 B.C.), many civilizations in **Europe** began using bronze to make jewelry. Warriors wore neck rings, or "torques," as protective charms. Women were adorned in bronze spiral bracelets. Some Europeans of the upper class also decorated themselves in bronze jewelry to show their wealth and power.

STAINED GLASS

Materials:

small squares of colored tissue paper
black construction paper
scissors
waxed paper
liquid starch
paintbrush
masking tape

1. **Fold** black paper in half and **cut** out a border.

2. **Cut** waxed paper to fit "window." **Tape** to back.

3. **Overlap** tissue squares on top of waxed paper. **Brush** with starch.

4. **Tape** several "windows" together. **Hang**.

tape together on back

Many of the oldest stained glass windows are found in cathedrals in **Italy**. Some windows date back to the Middle Ages, when flat glass could only be made in small pieces. Strips of lead held the pieces together. Artists eventually created huge windows that were made from thousands of tiny glass pieces. These windows told "picture stories" to people who were unable to read.

STENCILING

Materials:

stencils
sponge pieces
masking tape
acrylic paints in shallow bowls
large terra cotta flower pot

1. **Tape** stencils on pot.

2. **Dip** sponge into paint.

3. **Dab** paint over one section (over stencils).

4. **Repeat** using other colors. Let **dry**.

People from the Bavarian section of **Germany** brought the art of stenciling to America. Traveling painters went from town to town decorating the walls, furniture, and floors of inns and farmhouses with stencil patterns. Favorite designs were colorful flowers, plants, animals, and simple scenes.

THAUMATROPE

Materials:

3" circle cut from poster board
markers
string
scissors

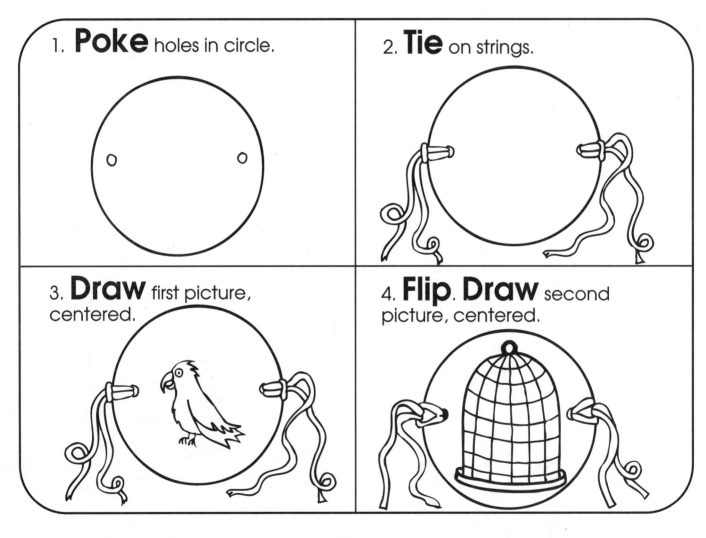

1. **Poke** holes in circle.

2. **Tie** on strings.

3. **Draw** first picture, centered.

4. **Flip. Draw** second picture, centered.

In **England**, people of all ages enjoyed drawing pictures on thaumatropes, "miracle-turn" puzzles that trick the eye. Dr. Paris, an Englishman, invented this amazing toy. By rolling the strings back and forth between the thumb and first finger, the pictures on both sides of the circle appear as one. The eye retains the image of the first picture long enough for a second image to be superimposed upon it.

TIE-DYE

Materials:

cotton cloth
rubber bands
cold-water fabric dye
bucket
water
wooden spoon

sink
hanger or clothesline

1. **Bunch** fabric and **wrap** with rubber bands.

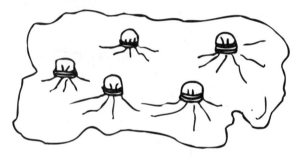

2. **Soak** cloth in dye. **Rinse**.

3. **Remove** rubber bands.

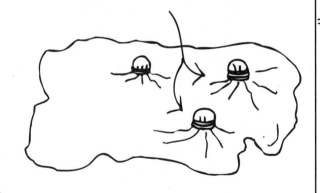

4. **Hang** to dry.

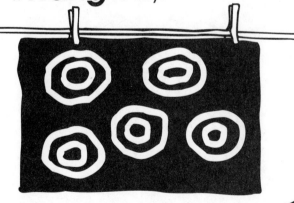

In **Nigeria**, mothers teach their daughters the art of creating traditional African patterns in tie-dyed cloth. Nigerian peddlers (most often women) are called "Petty Traders." They travel through northern Africa selling their tie-dyed cloth and other local handmade crafts. Clothing in this hot climate is usually colorful and free-flowing.

Materials:

oblong-shaped paper plate (Chinette type)

papier mâché (newspaper strips, paste mix of water and flour or glue)

materials for mask features: egg carton cups, cardboard tubes, plastic lids, heavy twine, corks, sticks, etc.

raffia
glue
masking tape
hole punch
scissors
tempera paint
paintbrushes

1. **Tape** and **glue** materials to plate to create features.

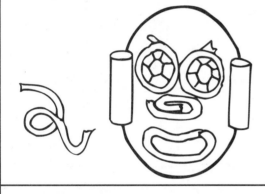

2. **Papier mâché**. Let **dry**.

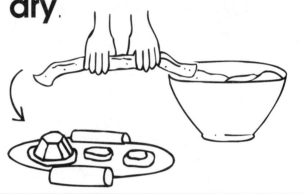

3. **Paint** and let **dry**.

4. **Punch** holes. **Tie** on raffia.

Masks were an important part of tribal ceremonies in **Africa**. Some African masks had exaggerated animal features. Mask-makers added bulging eyes, distorted noses and mouths, pointed fangs and horns, and elaborate hair. Mask decorations included pebbles, grasses, feathers, and animal claws and teeth. Many masked characters also appeared in traditional African myths and legends.

VICTORIAN BOUQUET

Materials:

wildflowers and leaves that have
been pressed between pages of
an old, heavy book
soft brush
thin ribbon

picture frame (or one made from
cardboard)
paper cut to fit frame
glue

1. **Arrange** dried bouquet on paper.

2. **Brush** glue onto backs of flowers and stems. **Press** down.

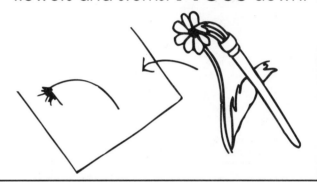

3. **Tie** and **glue** on bow.

4. **Frame**.

Women in **England** preserved fresh flowers by pressing the delicate petals and leaves in a book. The bouquet was dried between the book's pages and then placed on fine paper. The flowers were often framed in glass and used on floral tea trays or hung on the wall for decoration.

*Note: Pick wildflowers only in areas where it is allowed—any delicate flower will press well.

ZULU COIL ART

Materials:

cardboard (place mat size)
burlap (blue)
twine or yarn (yellow, brown, and rust)
scissors
glue

1. **Glue** burlap to cardboard to cover.

2. **Make** coils of yarn.

3. **Apply** circles of glue to burlap.

4. **Press** yarn coils to glue.

The Zulu tribe of southern **Africa** created richly colored and textured wall hangings. Plant and vegetable fibers were used to make colored dyes of indigo blue, sunny yellow, earthen tan, and rust. Cotton strands were then dyed, coiled, and sewn onto an unbleached cloth to decorate the walls of the mud huts.

BARK PAINTING

Materials:

white paper
piece of wood
brown crayon (remove paper)
markers (red, black, yellow, and white)

1. **Rub** crayon on paper over wood grain.

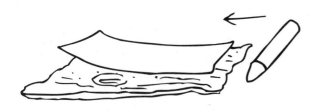

2. **Draw** animal. **Divide** into sections.

3. **Draw** lines and dots inside sections.

4. **Color**.

For thousands of years, the aborigine tribes of **Australia** painted pictures of animals such as the kangaroo on prepared tree bark. Some artists etched designs in the blackened surface with their thumbnails. Others chewed the end of a stick to use as a brush.

Materials:

stove
teapot
water
large shallow pan
white cotton fabric
cold-water dye

muffin tin
bucket
crayon pieces
paintbrushes (one per color)
iron (on warm setting)
paper towels

1. **Pour** hot water into pan under tin to melt crayons.

2. **Paint** picture with melted wax on cloth.

3. **Crumple** cloth. **Soak** cloth in dye.

4. **Iron** with wax side down between paper towels.

Batik (bah-TEEK) means "wax painting" in the language of the people of Java in **Indonesia**. The Javanese artist collects wax from wild beehives in the forest. Dyes are made by crushing the roots and leaves of native plants. Wax is applied to the fabric. Then the cloth is dyed and dried, and the wax is removed by scrubbing with warm water.

*Note: Be sure an adult helps when using an iron.

BLOSSOM PAINTING

Materials:

watercolor paints
paintbrush
white paper
cup of water

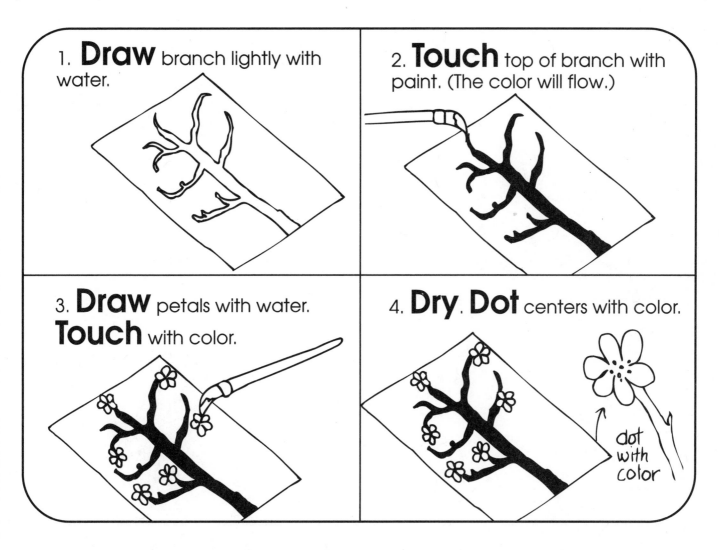

1. **Draw** branch lightly with water.

2. **Touch** top of branch with paint. (The color will flow.)

3. **Draw** petals with water. **Touch** with color.

4. **Dry**. **Dot** centers with color.

dot with color

Artists in **Japan** placed their paper on the floor and worked on their knees. They created simple paintings with delicate brush strokes and often used ink rather than paint. Many people in Japan today paint a single flower blossom on a letter that is written to a friend or loved one.

CHARM BRACELET

Materials:

colored clay (self-hardening)
hairpin
leather strips or string
scissors
small paintbrush

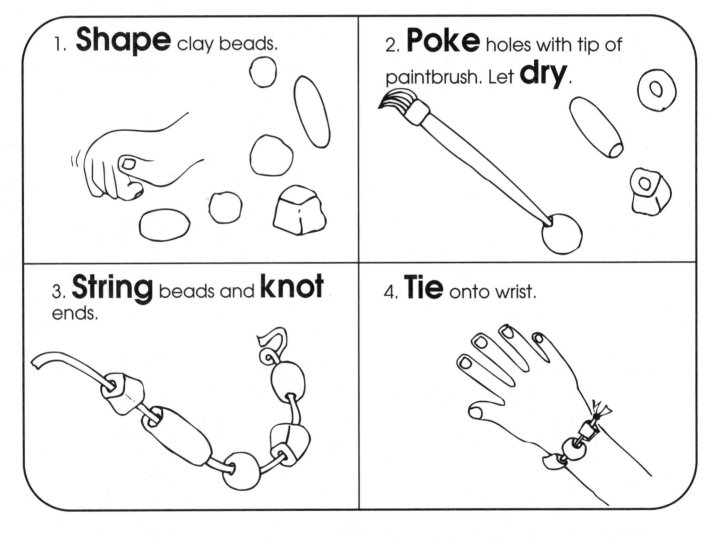

1. **Shape** clay beads.

2. **Poke** holes with tip of paintbrush. Let **dry**.

3. **String** beads and **knot** ends.

4. **Tie** onto wrist.

In northern **India**, men and women strung beads together to make charm bracelets. They believed that charms held magical powers that protected them against harm. Beads, which have been thought to have spiritual value, have also been traded and exchanged as currency in many cultures.

DIDJERIDOO

Materials:

wrapping paper tube
paint
paintbrush
scissors
foil

1. **Cut** three slits in both ends. **Flatten**.

2. **Paint** outside. Let **dry**.

3. Tightly **cover** one end with foil.

4. **Scrunch** foil around tube.

The didjeridoo is a musical instrument made by the aborigines in **Australia**. It is made from a long branch that has been hollowed out by ants. Lines and symbols are painted onto the branch. Then the didjeridoos are played at music-filled ceremonial dances, called "corroborees." The didjeridoo is played by blowing into it as one would a trumpet, with tight, vibrating lips and puffed-out cheeks.

Materials:

clay (self-hardening)
candle (birthday type)
paint (earthen colors)
paintbrush

1. **Roll** clay into a ball.

2. **Form** shallow bowl.

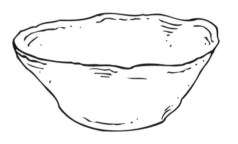

3. **Push** candle into bottom. Let **dry**.

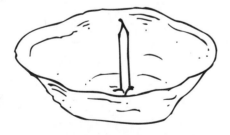

4. **Paint** bowl.

The people of **India** celebrate the New Year with the "Festival of Lights," or Divali (De-WAH-lee). On this evening, earthen oil lamps glow in the windows of every home. These lamps, or diyas (DEE-yahs), light the way and welcome Lakshmi, the goddess of wealth and good luck. Families also receive special sweets and play games of chance amid the noise of firecrackers popping in the streets.

DRAGON KITE

Materials:

copy paper sheet (8 1/2" x 11")
straw (plastic)
string
tissue paper strips in many colors
markers
tape

glue
scissors
hole punch

1. **Fold** center of copy paper to form ridge. **Color**.

← fold

2. **Tape** back seam and straw.

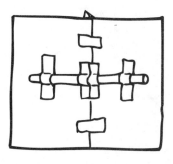

3. **Glue** on tissue paper strips.

4. **Punch** hole and **tie** string.

It is believed that the first kite was invented in **China** nearly 3,000 years ago. This kite-building craft was later shared with other Asian countries. Today, kite creations are endless. There are fighting kites, acrobatic kites, simple kites, and elaborate stacked-box kites. One favorite in China is the dragon kite.

Materials:

6" circle cut from file folder
12" strip cut from file folder
eight 8" tissue paper squares
   (cut from two different colors)
glue stick
string

scissors
stapler
hole punch

1. **Glue** paper corners.

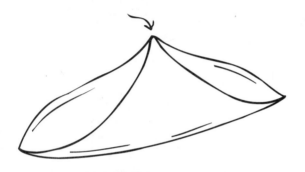

2. **Glue** bottom corners to circle.

3. **Staple** strip. **Punch** holes. **Cut/tie** string.

4. **Glue** paper corners onto strip.

glue corners

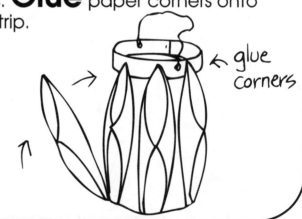

In **Iran**, the celebration Charshanbeh Soore (char-shan-BAY so-RAY), which means "Wednesday Celebration," falls on the last Wednesday of the year. On this day, Iranian families make a lantern called a fanus (fa-NOOS). At night, children carry the lanterns from house to house to get treats from their neighbors. Later, during fireworks displays, families make a special wish for good health for the coming year.

FATIMAS HAND CHARM

Materials:

copper wire (18-24 gauge)
wire cutters or heavy-duty scissors
hammer

1. **Bend** wire to form a thumb shape.

2. **Shape** fingers. **Snip** wire, leaving length for loop.

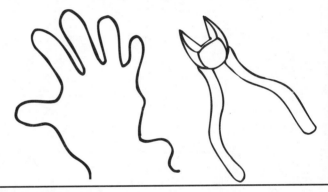

3. **Twist** ends. **Form** loop.

4. **Pound** flat.

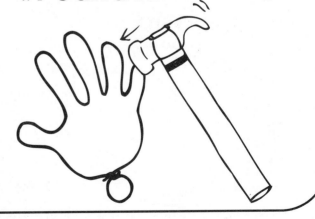

In the **Middle East**, the hasma, or fatimas hand, is considered to be a symbol of protection. Even today, the fatimas is commonly worn as a jewelry charm on a necklace. Some people believe that it has the power to ward off the "evil eye." Other people wear a symbol of the hand for good luck and fortune.

Materials:

card stock
tissue paper (folded)
string
stapler
scissors
markers

hole punch
glue

1. **Draw** and **cut** fish from tissue paper.

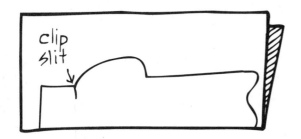

2. **Color** both sides of fish.

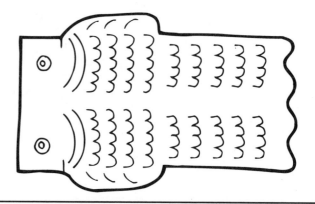

3. **Apply** glue. Press on card stock strip. **Fold** fish.

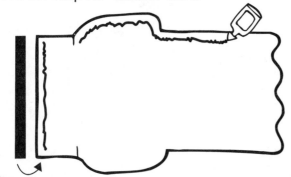

4. **Staple** mouth. **Punch** holes. **Tie** string.

Families in **Japan** celebrate "Children's Day," called Kodomo-no-hi (KOH-doh-moh-noh-HEE), by flying carp-shaped flags from tall bamboo poles. Carp must be strong and determined to swim upstream against the current. These fish symbolize courage, stamina, and the ability to overcome difficulties. Japanese families respect these qualities and teach them to their children.

HMONG STORY CLOTH

Materials:

simple story
white cotton fabric
blue cotton fabric
acrylic paints
paintbrushes
pencil

black marker
glue
scissors

1. **Cut** blue border. **Glue** to white fabric.

2. **Sketch** scenes lightly with pencil.

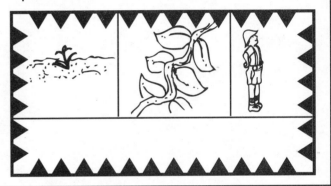

3. **Paint**.

4. **Write** words to story.

Once upon a time, a magic bean . . .

The **Hmong** (MUNG) people migrated from Tibet and Nepal through China. They settled in small villages scattered throughout parts of Vietnam, Laos, and Thailand. The Hmong women skillfully hand-sewed fabric, and shared their history through their needlework. Hmong story cloths tell of ancient legends, mountain life in Laos, and the war in Southeast Asia.

Materials:

paper towel tube
white paper
tape
scissors
paint
paintbrush
crayons

1. **Flatten** the cardboard tube.

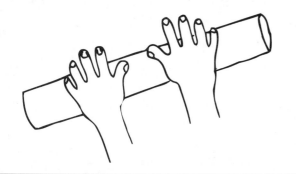

2. **Cover** with white paper. **Trim** and **tape**.

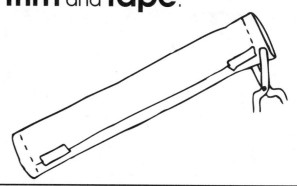

3. **Color** and **paint**. Let **dry**.

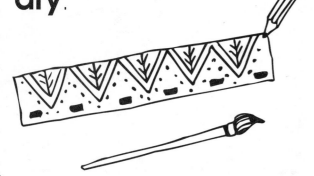

4. **Deliver** the stick with an oral message.

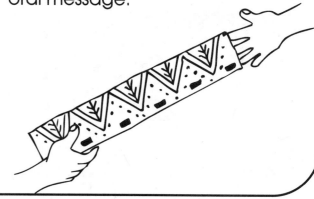

In **Australia**, each aborigine tribe selected several young men to serve as messengers. The young men carried special sticks carved with meaningful symbols by the elders. A messenger often traveled a long distance to reach another tribe. He delivered his news orally, and left the stick as a reminder of the arrangement.

MONEY BOX

Materials:

container with plastic lid (instant gourmet coffee containers work well)
thick yarn
tacky glue
scissors
plastic knife (to make slit)

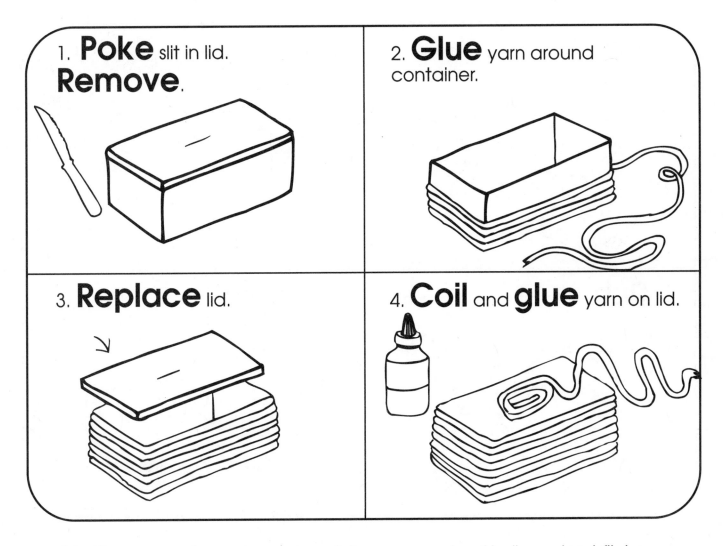

1. **Poke** slit in lid. **Remove**.

2. **Glue** yarn around container.

3. **Replace** lid.

4. **Coil** and **glue** yarn on lid.

Primitive money boxes in western **Asia** were made of hollowed-out flint or molded clay. As soon as people began to use and exchange money, they realized that they needed a place to save their coins. For many years, people crafted money boxes out of wood or pottery. By the late 1880's, however, mechanical money boxes with moving parts that "snatched" the coins were made of metal or cast iron.

Materials:

white paper
larger colored paper
peeled crayon
relief (use any flat object with a
    raised surface such as a plaque,
    coin, key, or leaf)

cloth (to clean surface of relief if dirty)
masking tape
glue or rubber cement

1. **Clean** surface of relief.

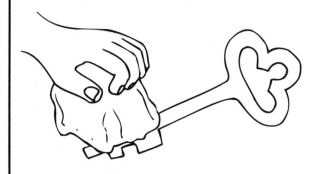

2. **Tape** white paper over relief.

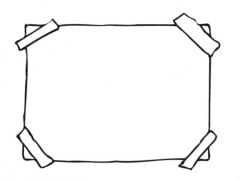

3. **Rub** with flat side of crayon.

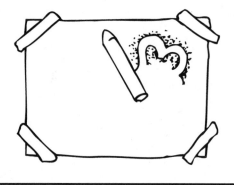

4. **Mount** on colored paper.

People in **China** made rubbings from famous reliefs. First, they covered the relief's surface with thin, moistened paper. Next, they used a dry brush to force the paper into each nook and cranny. Once the paper was dry, semi-solid pieces of ink were rubbed lightly over the paper. The raised impression turned black, creating an exact replica of the relief. Reliefs were considered to be the beginning of the art of printing.

SAND STORY

Materials:

scratch paper
pencil
small sheet of sandpaper
crayons
dry iron (on warm setting)
newspaper

1. **Create** symbols and meanings for story on paper.

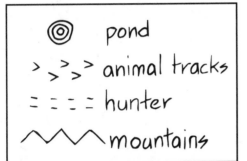

2. **Color** picture on sandpaper.

3. **Lay** wax side down on newspaper.

4. **Press** with iron.

For more than 30,000 years, the aborigine tribes of **Australia** used the ground as their canvas. They cleared and stamped a flat ground area to make their paintings. Artists created their designs with symbols passed down from elder tribesmen. Paintings told of spiritual knowledge, medical cures, and hunting stories.

*Note: Be sure an adult helps when using an iron.

SARIMANOK

Materials:

file folder
"secret" note
scissors
markers or crayons
glue
glitter
tape

sarimanok pattern

1. **Copy** pattern onto fold of file folder. **Cut** out.

2. **Decorate** bird with markers and glitter.

3. **Fold** note inside fish. **Tape** fish to beak.

4. **Bend** base of bird. **Stand**.

In the **Philippines**, Sarimanok (sari-ma-NEWK) means "bird-like." It is a symbol of good luck. A legend tells of a tribal leader who put a secret message in the small fish that the Sarimanok carried in its beak. The bird delivered the note to a loved one far away. This beautiful bird remains an important part of the Filipino culture, and represents such qualities as love, courage, and freedom.

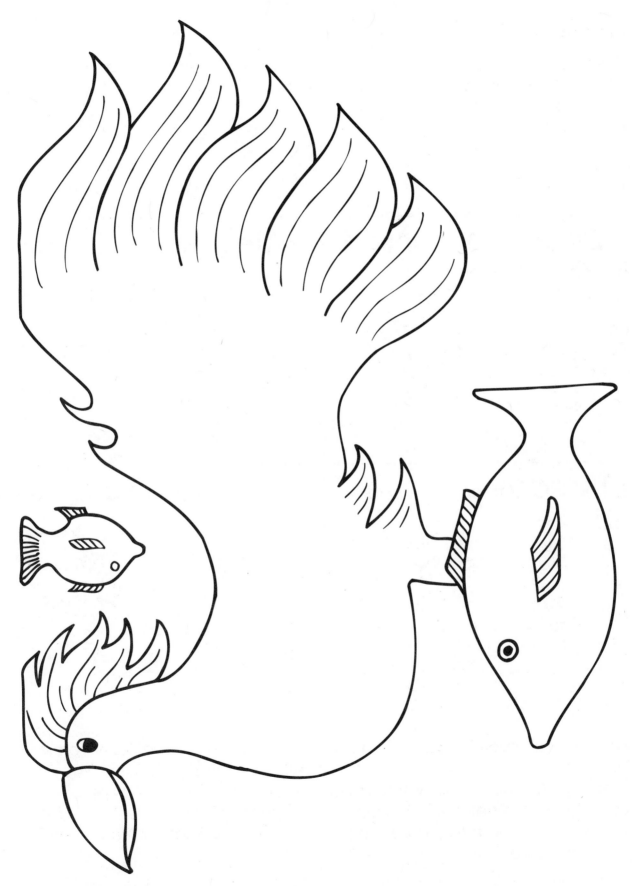

Materials:

6 pre-cut fan sticks (cut from a file folder) with 3 small holes in each
large needle threaded with heavy thread
paper fastener
clear tape
markers
perfume or cologne (spray)

1. **Decorate** and **insert** fastener into stacked sticks.

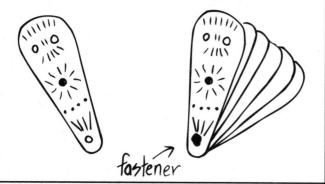

2. **Tie** thread onto top strip.

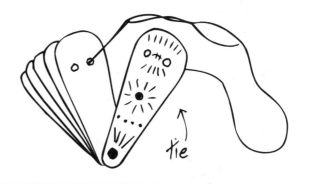

3. **Thread** throughout and **tie**.

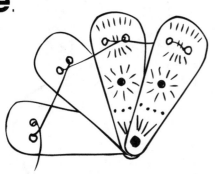

4. **Tape** backs. **Spray** with scent.

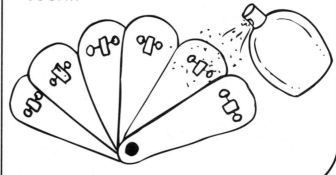

Artists in **Malaysia** carved fans from sandalwood trees of the Bandi Forest. After carving and smoothing the fan sticks, the artists pierced tiny holes to create patterns. The fans were dipped into water before being used. This brought out the naturally scented oils in the wood. The handles of the fans were carved and the fans were given poetic names such as "Thundery-weather Flower."

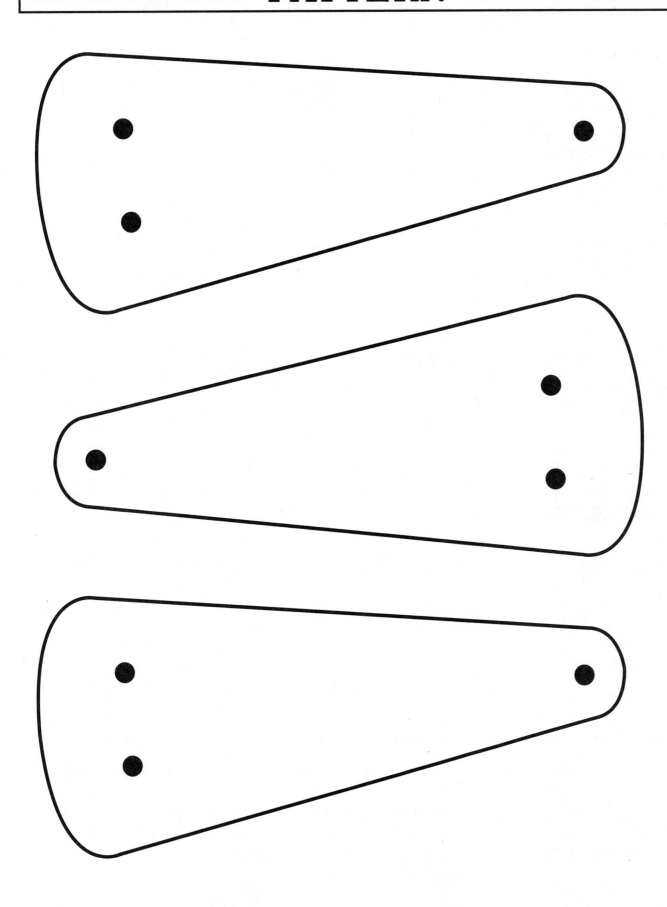

SHADOW PUPPET

Materials:

file folder
pre-cut dragon pattern
chopsticks
paper fasteners
markers

scissors
masking tape
pencil

1. **Trace** shape.

2. **Cut** out and **color**.

3. **Attach** movable parts.

4. **Tape** on sticks.

Wajang-kulit is a shadow-puppet show in **Indonesia**. The puppeteer usually sits on the floor between a white screen and a lamp. When he holds up the puppet, a moving shadow image appears on the screen. The puppets are often dragons or animals. The artist constructs the movable puppet bodies from leather and then paints them in bright colors, even though the shadow is all that is seen.

SLAP FLAP HAT

Materials:

roll of wide paper (3' length)
scissors
masking tape

1. **Lay** section of paper over head.

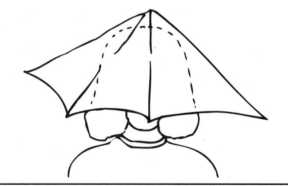

2. **Hold** paper for friend to **tape**.

3. **Lift** off head and **trim** front brim.

4. **Trim** back flaps.

In **Australia**, many children protect their skin from the blazing afternoon sun by wearing hats with flaps. The Australian government's mascot, Sid the Sea Gull, encourages everyone to "slip" on a shirt, "slop" on some sunscreen, and "slap" on a hat before going outdoors. Some schools even require children to wear hats during recess and lunch. So . . . slip, slop, slap, and be safe, mate!

STONE RELIEF

Materials:

shoe box lid
clay
plaster of Paris
plastic utensils (for carving)

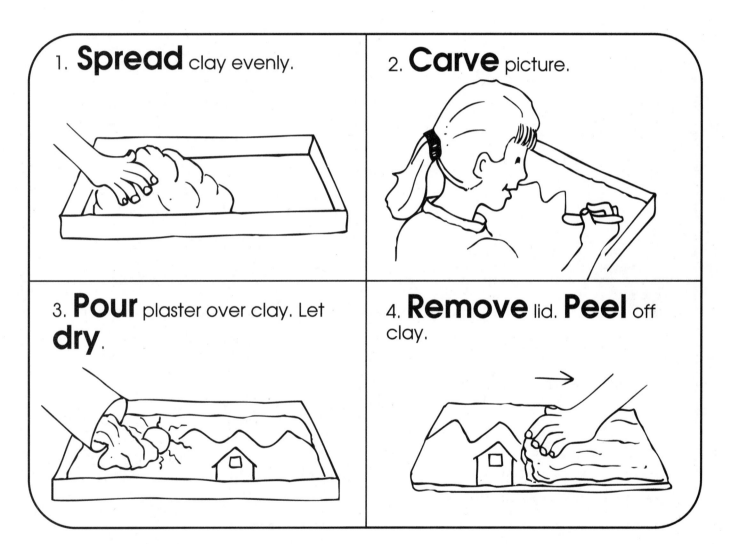

1. **Spread** clay evenly.

2. **Carve** picture.

3. **Pour** plaster over clay. Let **dry**.

4. **Remove** lid. **Peel** off clay.

Emperors in **China** used reliefs (pictures or words carved into stone) to teach the wise sayings of Confucius, an ancient Chinese philosopher. These carved sayings were displayed in front of the Imperial School for all to see. The reliefs, known as the Stone Classics, became famous works of art. Students made rubbings from the tablets, a fast way of copying and passing along the words of wisdom.

Materials:

small box lid
string (parameter of box four times)
tape (transparent)
scissors

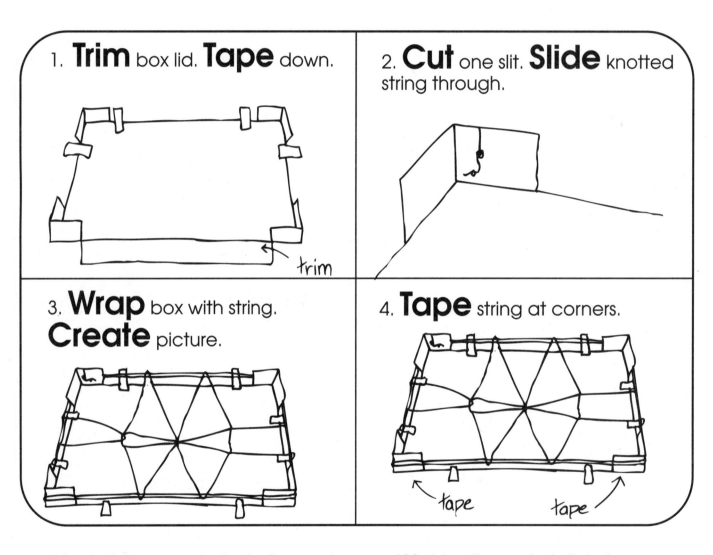

1. **Trim** box lid. **Tape** down.

trim

2. **Cut** one slit. **Slide** knotted string through.

3. **Wrap** box with string. **Create** picture.

4. **Tape** string at corners.

tape   tape

Aborigine women in **Australia** create over 400 string figures to tell stories with. The storyteller sometimes uses her teeth or toes to assist in making these "cat's cradle"-type designs or two women may work together to make complicated figures. They must practice the sequence of steps until the pattern is memorized. The string used by the aborigines is made from bark fiber that is easy to carry when the tribe travels.

TANABATA

Materials:

branch
pencil
note-sized piece of paper
scissors
hole punch
yarn

1. **Punch** a hole in paper.

2. **Write** a wish.

I wish for good health and happiness for my family.

3. **Thread** yarn through hole.

I wish for good health and happiness for my family.

4. **Tie** to the branch.

In **Japan**, Tanabata (Tahn-uh-bah-tuh), or "Festival of the Stars," is held on July 7th. This celebration is based on a legend about stars in the night sky that meet only once a year. Children in Japan celebrate by wishing for good health and fortune for their families—and possibly for toys for themselves. The "wishes" are displayed on bamboo in front of the children's houses for all to see.

Materials:

large black square of paper
white chalk
background paper
ruler
scissors
glue

1. **Fold** black paper into triangle. **Fold** again.

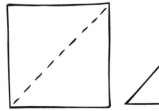 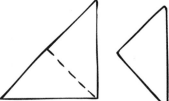

2. **Open** and **fold** in half. **Fold** in half again.

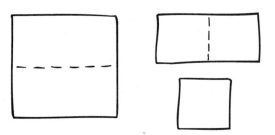

3. **Draw** pattern lines in chalk using ruler to make shapes.

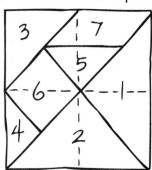

4. **Cut**, **create**, and **glue** to background.

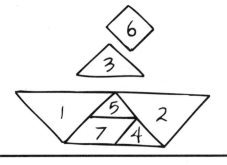

A tangram is a fascinating seven-piece puzzle that is called Qi-Qiao Baan (CHEE-chee-ow Bahn) in **China**. The simple geometric shapes are cut from one large square. They can be fit together to create more than a thousand different designs! Tangram puzzles can be almost anything: people, boats, animals, airplanes, complete action stories, as well as the ABCs.

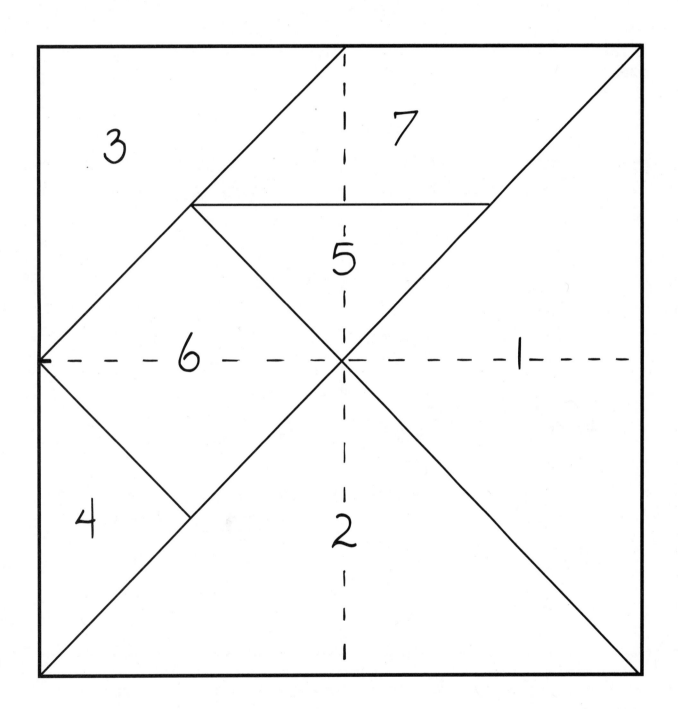

TREASURE BOX

Materials:

clay
pencil
string
scissors

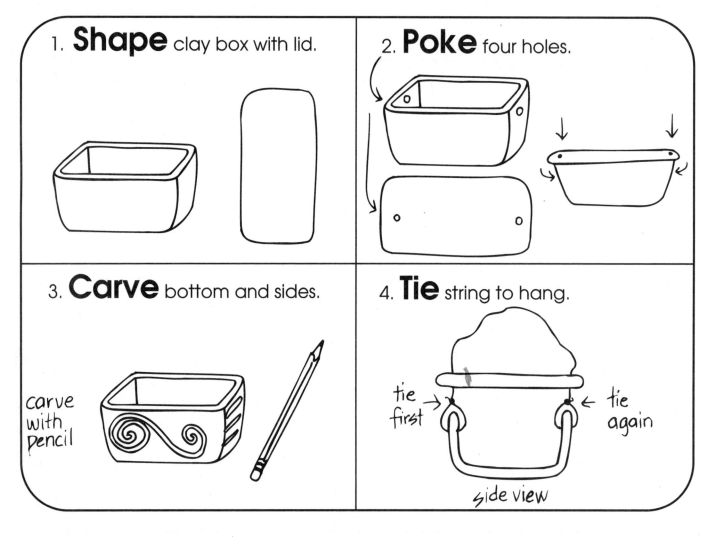

1. **Shape** clay box with lid.

2. **Poke** four holes.

3. **Carve** bottom and sides.

carve with pencil

4. **Tie** string to hang.

tie first →

← tie again

side view

The **Maori** craftsmen are famous for their beautiful wood carvings. The treasure boxes, known as waka-huia, were used to hold precious objects, such as jade ornaments, combs, and prized feathers. These valued boxes were hung from high rafters for safekeeping. A Maori carver always completed the elaborate work on the bottom of his treasure box first because this was the part in view.

AYAGAK

Materials:

paper tube
string
scissors
stick or dowel

1. **Poke** small hole in paper tube.

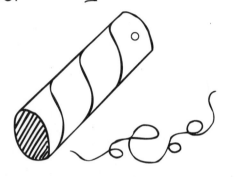

2. **Push** string through hole.

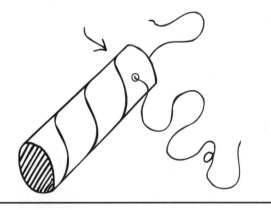

3. **Tie** large knot.

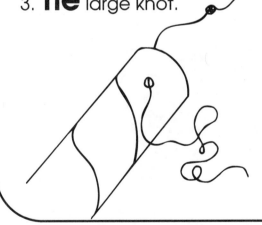

4. **Wrap** string around stick and **knot**.

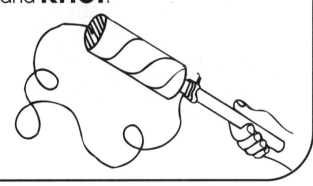

Inuit children of the United States and Canada played many simple games to develop their hand-eye coordination. These games prepared them for hunting, while providing indoor fun during the long winter months. The Inuit used seal bone and walrus sinew to make the ayagak, a version of the stick-and-hole toy used by many world cultures.

CARIOCA MASK

Materials:

wide masking tape
poster board
long stick or dowel
markers
glitter

curling ribbon
glue
scissors

1. **Cut** mask shape.

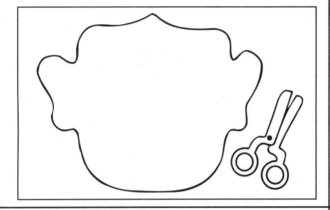

2. **Tape** stick to back.

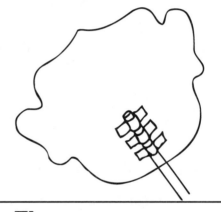

3. **Decorate** with markers and glitter.

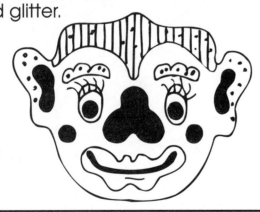

4. **Tie** on curly ribbons.

The Carioca Festival in **Brazil** is a time of feasts, masquerade parties, and parades. Local merchants decorate the city with clown and devil masks that sway from high-flying poles and lamp posts. The Brazilian samba beat fills the air and costumed characters dance through the streets during this wild "People of Rio" festival that lasts for three days and nights.

Materials:

cloth fabric
textured fabric remnants
cardboard rectangle
scissors
glue
yarn

1. **Glue** cloth to cardboard.

2. **Cut** shapes from remnants.

3. **Glue** on shapes.

4. **Glue** on yarn.

Women in **Colombia** create colorful scenes with cloth applique and then add detail with embroidery stitches. "Applique" comes from the French word "appliquer," which means "to put on or apply." To applique, the edges of cutout fabric shapes are turned under and then sewn to a background cloth to make a picture. The pictures are often of places well loved by the artists.

DANCE CUFFS

Materials:

brown paper bag
large bold-color markers
scissors
stapler
ruler

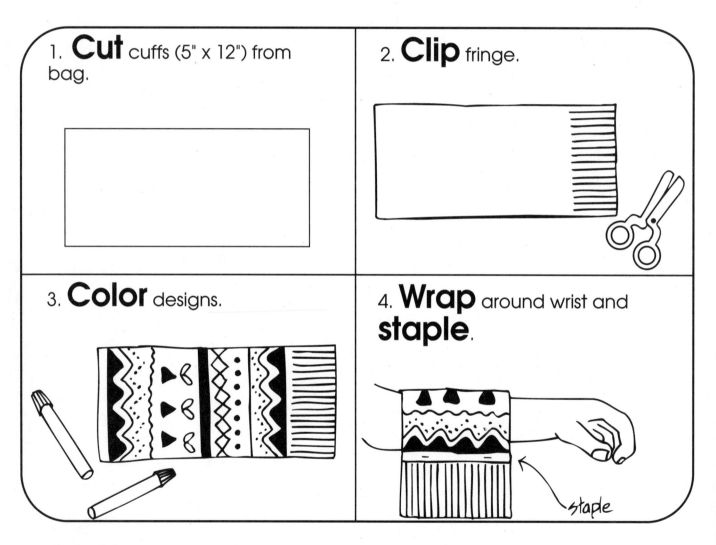

1. **Cut** cuffs (5" x 12") from bag.

2. **Clip** fringe.

3. **Color** designs.

4. **Wrap** around wrist and **staple**.

staple

Native American men of the Great Plains performed ceremonial dances wearing horned headpieces, ankle bells, and fringed arm cuffs made of animal skins. During the Buffalo Dance, two dancers pawed the ground and tossed their heads to show respect for the mighty buffalo. Since the buffalo provided the tribe with its main source of food, clothing, and shelter, the men also danced to ask their gods for help before a big hunt.

FRINGED CAPE

Materials:

roll of wide paper (3' length)
paint
paintbrush
scissors

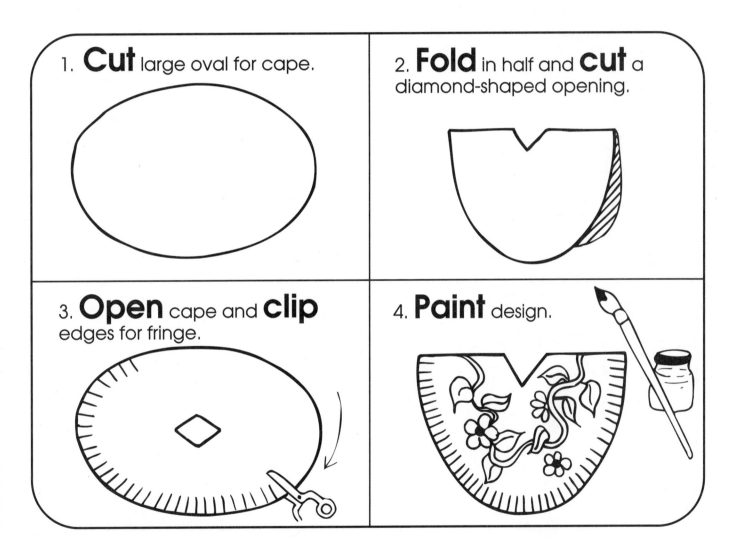

1. **Cut** large oval for cape.

2. **Fold** in half and **cut** a diamond-shaped opening.

3. **Open** cape and **clip** edges for fringe.

4. **Paint** design.

Eastern Woodland **Native Americans** wore heavily beaded floral-theme capes of fringed leather when dancing at ceremonies. The capes were worn for spiritual power, as well as warmth. Medicinal items, such as animal claws and bird feathers, were sometimes attached. Today, capes may still be worn during traditional Native American dances.

HULA SKIRT

Materials:

yarn lengths (long enough to wrap around waist and tie)
package of crepe paper (green or natural color)
scissors
2 chairs

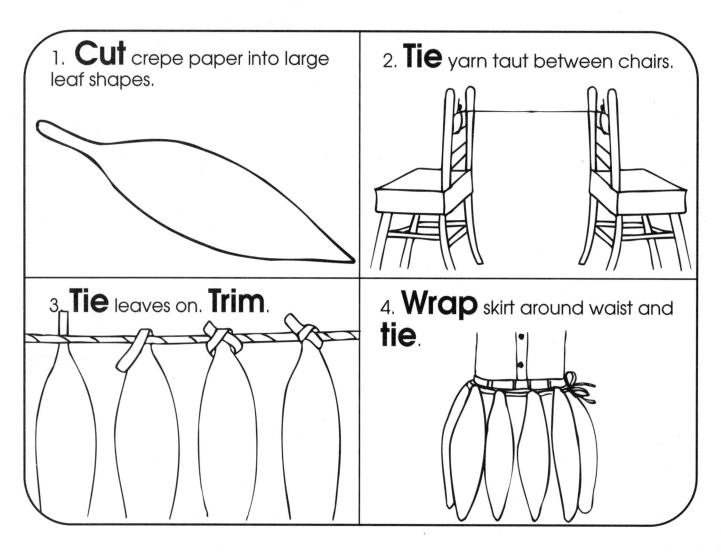

1. **Cut** crepe paper into large leaf shapes.

2. **Tie** yarn taut between chairs.

3. **Tie** leaves on. **Trim**.

4. **Wrap** skirt around waist and **tie**.

In the ancient **Hawaiian Islands**, the hula (HOO-lah) dance took the place of written language. The hula is still an important part of the Hawaiian culture. At a feast called a luau (LOO-ow), girls wear leis and hula skirts made of ti (TEE) leaves. To ukulele and drum music, hula dancers sway their hips from side to side. They use their arms and hands to describe the beauty of the islands and tell their native history.

INUIT GOGGLES

Materials:

paper towel tube
scissors
pencil
elastic
hole punch

1. **Cut** tube in half lengthwise.

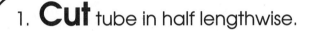

2. **Flatten. Trim** edges of tube.

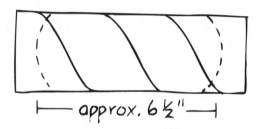

approx. 6 ½"

3. **Mark** and **cut** eye slits.

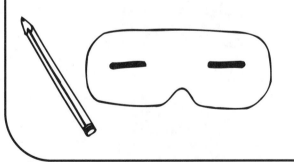

4. **Punch** holes. **Tie** on elastic.

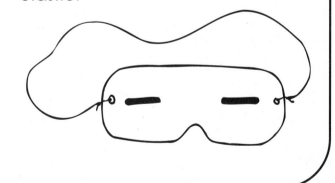

The Ice Age hunters of North America, who lived in a region now part of Canada, carved snow goggles from ivory, bone, and driftwood. The viewing slits in the goggles were necessary to block the glare of the sun reflecting off the frozen terrain. The modern day inhabitants of the region are called **Inuits**. "Inuit" means "the people." They are skillful hunters.

ᛞᛟᛠᛞᛠ IROQUOIS SUN MASK ᛞᛠᛞᛠᛞ

Materials:

corn husk strips (water soaked, towel dried)
file folder
paint (yellow, green, orange)
paintbrushes
scissors
hole punch

1. **Cut** mask shape, eyes, and mouth from folder.

2. **Punch** holes on edge.

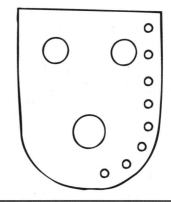

3. **Tie** on husks.

4. **Paint** mask.

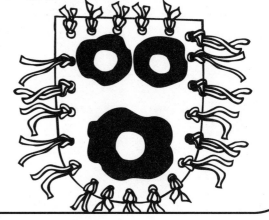

The **Iroquois** tribes braided masks from corn husks. These sun masks, or "husk faces," were worn during winter ceremonies to encourage a successful crop. The Iroquois tribes believed in a spiritual trio—the Spirit of the Corn, Spirit of the Beans, and Spirit of the Squashes. These three spirit sisters were known by the name De-o-ha'-ko, which means "our life."

KACHINA CROW MOTHER

Materials:

wood block (6" section of 2 x 4 board)
large empty spool
solid-color fabric remnant
markers
colored paper
scissors
glue

1. **Color** face on spool. **Glue** spool to wood.

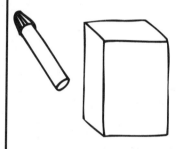

2. **Cut** and **glue** paper feathers and wings.

3. **Cut** and **design** fabric.

4. **Wrap** and **glue**.

Kachina (ka-CHEE-na) dolls, such as Crow Mother, are carved by the **Hopi tribe** of the American Southwest to teach children about the spirits of the wind, thunder, earth, and animals. Kachina spirits are believed to be helpful to the tribe. Dancers perform in full kachina costume to bring good spirits to earth. Many Hopi believe that Crow Mother is the mother of all kachinas.

KING KAMEHAMEHA HELMET

Materials:

roll of wide paper (3' length)
masking tape
scissors
stapler
glue

1. **Hold** paper for friend to **tape**.

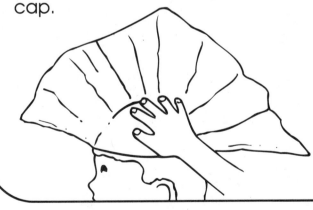

2. **Apply** glue to cap.

3. **Fold** sides up. **Press** to cap.

4. **Cut** helmet shape. **Staple**.

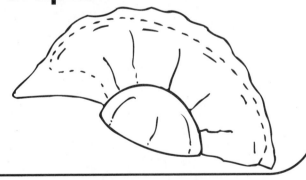

King Kamehameha (kah-MAY-hah-MAY-hah) united the people of all of the **Hawaiian Islands** to work together as one kingdom. During his time, chiefs and kings dressed in feathered cloaks and helmets for ceremonies and battles. To make the helmets, island craftsmen carefully wove the split roots of plants. For their kings, they adorned the spectacular helmets with feathers. Hawaiians honor King Kamehameha on June 11.

Materials:

string (approx. 3')
straws
tissue paper (yellow for ilima flowers; red for lehua blossoms; purple for
    mokihana berries; white for sweet gardenia flowers or white ginger; and
    yellow and white for plumeria blossoms)
hairpin
scissors

1. **Cut** flowers.

2. **Snip** straws into short pieces.

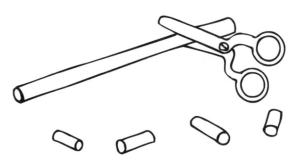

3. **Poke** holes in centers of flowers.

4. **String** flowers and straws. **Tie**.

A lei (LAY) is a necklace made of flowers native to the **Hawaiian Islands**. If a man gives a lei to a woman, it is an expression of love. If a friend gives a lei to another friend, it may mean "good news." When a native Hawaiian gives a lei to a visitor, it means "welcome." These delicate and sweet-smelling garlands are worn by both men and women in Hawaii.

Materials:

tight-weave burlap or woven fabric (cut to place mat size)
large needle threaded with embroidery thread
scissors
glue
chalk

1. **Draw** design.

2. **Stitch** along lines. **Tie** knot.

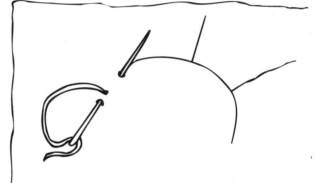

3. **Pull** burlap strings to create fringe.

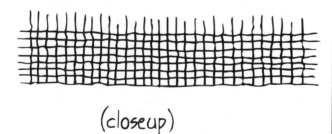

(closeup)

4. **Apply** line of glue to back.

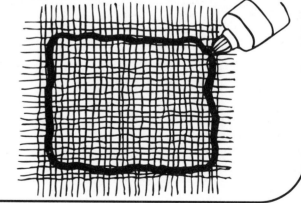

The ancient empires of what are now **Mexico and Peru** had no written language, so much of their history was lost or destroyed. The beauty and spirit of the artwork, however, reveals a highly developed culture. Artists and craftsmen created stone sculptures, masks of gold, and fired-clay pottery, as well as linear pictures of nature sewn in threads of wool and cotton.

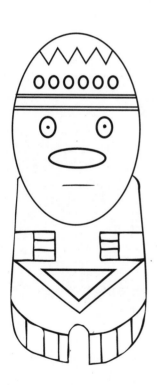

Materials:

solid-color fabric remnants (paper may be substituted)
pencil or chalk
scissors
glue
brush

1. **Draw** and **cut** simple shape.

2. **Brush** glue on back and **stick** to piece of fabric.

3. **Cut** around edge to make larger shape.

4. **Glue**, **cut**, and **stack** layers.

Molas are created by the Cuna Indians of the San Blas Islands off the coast of **Panama**. These art pieces are made by cutting through layers of colored cloth and then stitching the edges to create designs. Molas were once made in animal and plant shapes and used to decorate women's clothing. Today, molas are often framed or made into pins and worn as jewelry.

NAVAJO POTTERY

Materials:

clay
water

Optional:
pencil for carving
paint
paintbrush

---

1. **Flatten** ball of clay for bottom.

2. **Roll** strips of clay.

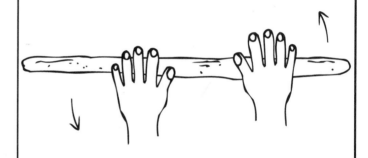

3. **Build** bowl by layering coils.

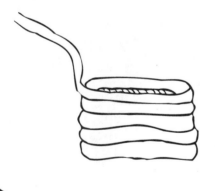

4. **Smooth** pot with wet hands.

Navajo (NAW-veh-ho) tribespeople of the American Southwest used clay from the earth to make pottery. These bowls, jugs, and pots were used for cooking and carrying water. The potter added designs to the moist clay by carving with sharpened sticks. After the clay dried, some artists colored their pottery with paints made from roots and plants that had been crushed and ground with stones.

OJIBWAY DREAM CATCHER

Materials:

wire hanger
flannel strips (brown or tan)
string
beads
feather
scissors

1. **Shape** wire into circle.

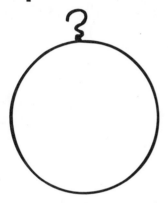

2. **Wrap** with flannel and **tie**.

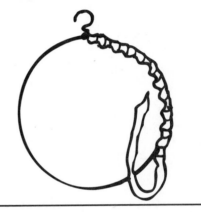

3. **Tie** on beaded strings to make web.

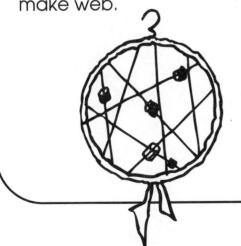

4. **Tie** on feather.

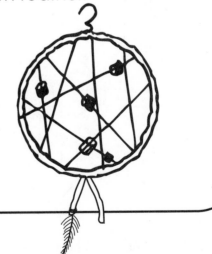

The **Ojibway** tribe (oh-JIB-way) of the Great Lakes and northern plains region believed that the night was filled with the spirits of dreams. They suspended dream catchers above the beds of their children. The web of the dream catchers trapped bad dream spirits. Good dreams passed through the web and floated down to the sleeping children.

Materials:

2 wooden sticks
yarn (bright colors)
glue
scissors

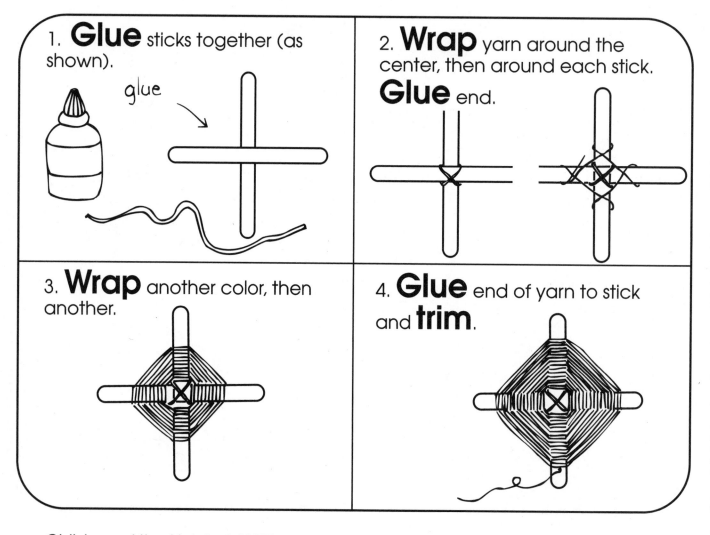

1. **Glue** sticks together (as shown).

glue

2. **Wrap** yarn around the center, then around each stick. **Glue** end.

3. **Wrap** another color, then another.

4. **Glue** end of yarn to stick and **trim**.

Children of the Huichol (WEE-chol) tribe in **Mexico** carry Ojo de Dios (O-ho deh DEE-os) wands on a special holiday. Ojo de Dios means "eye of god" in Spanish, and this design symbolizes the eye of the god Kauyumali. Huichol children hope that Kauyumali will see them with their wands and grant them healthy, long lives. Other children throughout Mexico hang the Ojo de Dios at the head of their beds for good luck.

PATCHWORK QUILT

Materials:

white card stock squares (8" x 8")
colored paper
roll of ribbon (to tie to quilt)
hole punch
scissors
glue

1. Cut shapes from colored paper.

2. Glue designs on white squares.

3. Punch holes in finished squares.

4. Tie with ribbons.

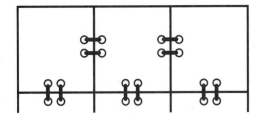

Patchwork quilts originated when housewives in **Colonial America** had to patch their worn comforters. Cloth was expensive and hard to get, so women saved good pieces of fabric from used clothes and linens. Then they cut and quilted each piece by hand into beautiful designs. The task was often shared among friends at a social gathering called a "quilting bee."

PENNSYLVANIA DUTCH EGG

Materials:

plastic egg
thin colored yarn (several colors)
glue
paintbrush
scissors

1. **Brush** glue on bottom section of egg.

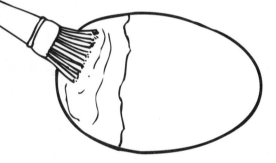

2. **Wrap** bottom section with yarn.

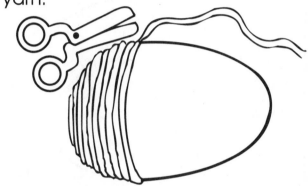

3. **Brush** glue on top section and **wrap** with yarn.

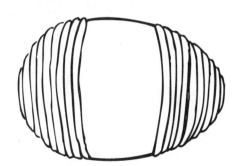

4. **Brush** glue and **coil** yarn in middle section.

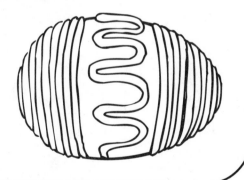

The art of egg decorating was brought to the United States by German immigrants who settled in the state of Pennsylvania. These immigrants became known as "**Pennsylvania Dutch**," because their word for German ("Deutsche") was misunderstood by other settlers as "Dutch." The artisans originally wrapped the soft center fibers of bisengraas, a tall, grass-like plant, around a blown-out egg to create a textured design.

PLATO DE COLORES

Materials:

scissors
paper plate (Chinette type)
string (or yarn)
paint (black and neon colors)
paintbrush
hole punch

1. **Punch** holes in plate.

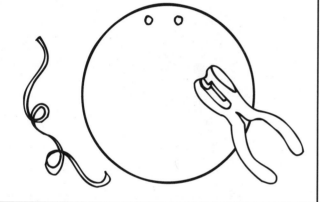

2. **Paint** plate solid black. Let **dry**.

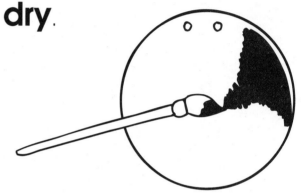

3. **Paint** flowers in neon colors.

4. **Hang** with string.

Festive colors are an important part of everyday life in **Mexico**. Brilliantly colored piñatas, baskets, clothing, and pottery brighten the shop windows. Artists hand-craft colorful "platos de colores" (PLAH-tohs deh coh-LOH-rehs), which means "colorful plate" in Spanish. Their creations are useful as dishes as well as works of art.

Materials:

empty, clean bleach bottle
two corks cut into halves
felt scraps (for eyes and ears)
pink chenille stick (coiled around pencil to shape for tail)
scissors
tacky glue

1. **Cut** slit in bottle top.

2. **Cut** and **glue** eyes and ears.

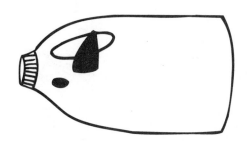

3. **Glue** corks on for feet.

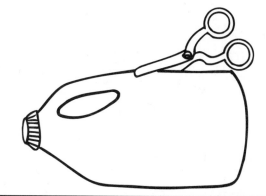

4. **Poke** hole and insert tail.

Children in **Colonial America**, who considered a penny a treasure, saved their coins in tin or glass kitchen jars. Eventually, a new kind of clay called "pygg" was introduced for making kitchenware. Children began putting their pennies in "piggy jars." Before long, these jars were manufactured to actually look like pigs and became known as "piggy banks."

RAISED-LINE JEWELRY

Materials:

card stock shape
long piece of string
glue
paintbrush
scissors
gold spray paint
jewelry pin

1. **Brush** glue on card stock shape.

2. **Press** string onto glue to make design.

3. **Spray paint** gold. Let dry.

4. **Glue** pin to back.

Goldsmiths in **ancient Colombia** created small sculptures and jewelry in two ways. One technique was to cast in gold. The other was to solder thick, gold wire to a flat sheet of gold to create raised-line details. This style was later used by the famous 20th-century artist Pablo Picasso in a series of cast gold pins.

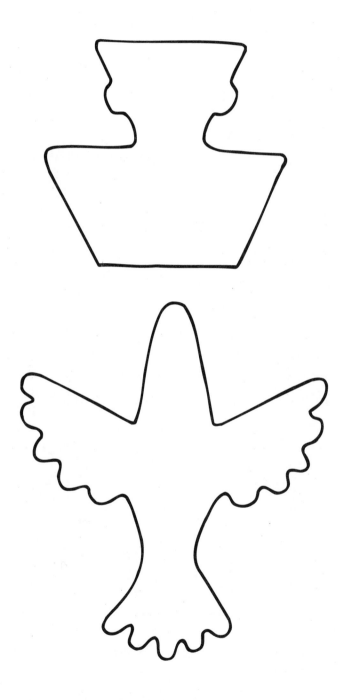

SERAPE

Materials:

roll of wide paper or fabric (6' length)
markers
scissors

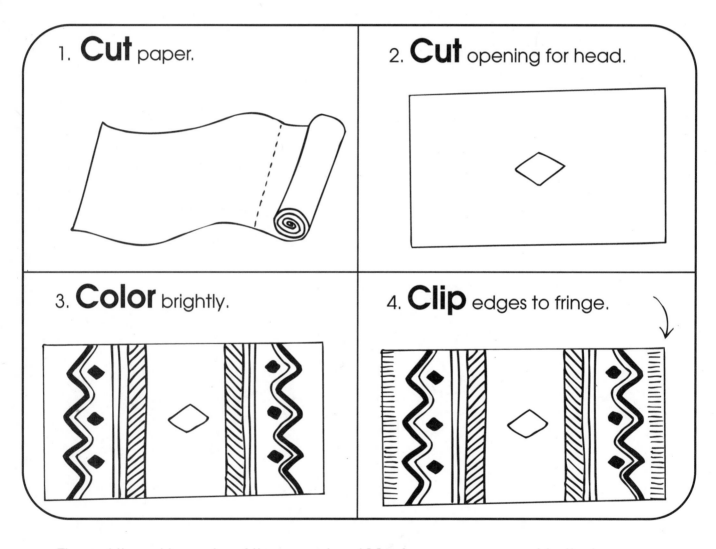

1. **Cut** paper.

2. **Cut** opening for head.

3. **Color** brightly.

4. **Clip** edges to fringe.

The spirit and beauty of the people of **Mexico** are apparent in their clothing, as well as in their arts and crafts. Men and boys wear a traditional garment called a serape (seh-RAH-pee), which is a brightly striped blanket that is worn over the shoulders like a poncho. Women wear a rebozo (re-BOH-zoh), which is similar to a shawl and bordered with colorful flowers.

SIOUX SHIELD

Materials:

cardboard circle (from pizza
   or bakery box)
heavy twine
feathers
pencil
paints

paintbrush
glue
scissors

1. **Poke** 4 holes in the circle.

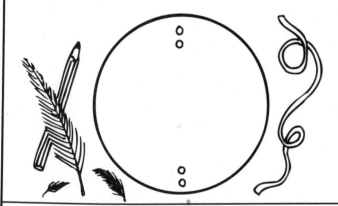

2. **Thread** twine through holes and **tie**.

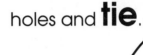

(side view)

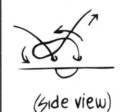

3. **Draw** and **paint** design.

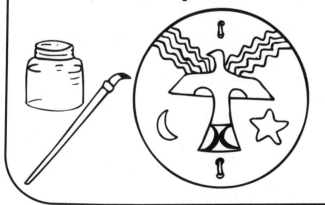

4. **Glue** feathers to design.

The **Sioux** were nomadic Native Americans who traveled across the northern plains hunting deer and buffalo. The Sioux shield, used in ceremonies and battle, was made of deer hide and painted with a spiritual symbol. A thunderbird with wavy lines above its wings symbolized thunder. A Sioux carrying the shield hoped to gain strength and protection from it.

TIN LANTERN

Materials:

tin can (filled with water and
   frozen solid)
white paper to fit can
black crayon
masking tape
hammer

large nail
folded towel
wide-based candle
glue
water

1. **Draw** pattern on paper. **Wrap** can and **tape**.

2. **Punch** holes on pattern lines.

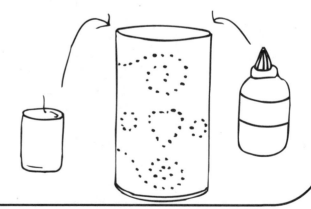

3. **Remove** paper and run can under warm water to **melt** ice.

4. **Glue** candle inside lantern.

Settlers in **Colonial America** depended on tin lanterns for light. Since there were no matches, these lanterns were used to light other fires. Families made their own lanterns or bought them from traveling peddlers ("tinkers") who carried tin goods between settlements.

TOTEM POLE

Materials:

4 to 6 cardboard box corners (wedges)
cardboard box flaps (cut for wings and beak of thunderbird)
plastic knife
paints
paintbrush

1. **Cut** 3" slits in bottom of all wedges.

2. **Fit** sections together.

3. **Cut** slits in thunderbird top. **Attach** wings and beak.

4. **Paint**.

The Story Pole of the Pacific Coast **Native Americans** of Alaska shows the tribe's desire to be in harmony with nature. They carved animals and spiritual symbols out of tree trunks to make totem poles; the thunderbird tops the pole and is symbolic of the "master of the skies." The Indians believed that these guardian spirits could offer help and protection. Totem poles were also used to teach tribal history to children.

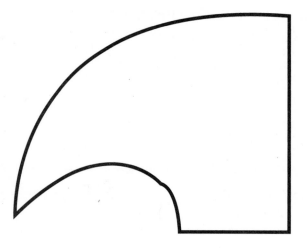

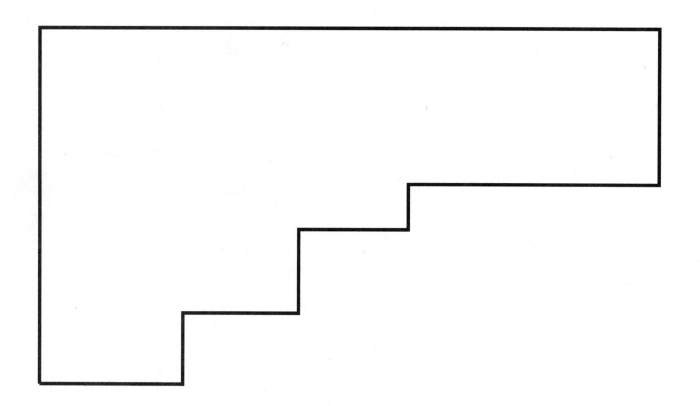

YARN PAINTING

Materials:

cardboard
yarn in bright colors
scissors
glue
paintbrush
pencil

1. **Draw** picture on cardboard.

2. **Brush** on glue.

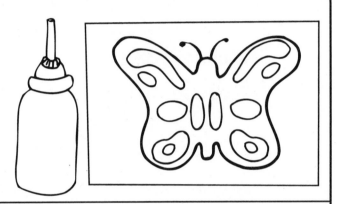

3. **Lay** yarn on lines.

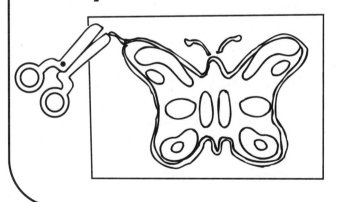

4. **Fill** in picture with yarn.

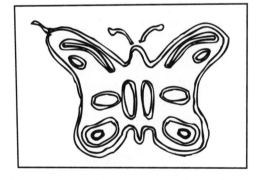

The Huichol (WEE-chol) live in an area of **Mexico** that is isolated by a high mountain range. The Huichols offer their art, such as yarn painting, to the gods. To make a yarn painting, the artist carves a design into wax and then presses yarn into the lines. The Huichol gods include Grandmother Growth (Nakawe), who is believed to bring water and a good harvest to the people and health and long life to the children.

RESOURCES

Aborigines of South-Eastern Australia: As They Were by Aldo Massola (Heinemann, 1971).

African Mythology by Geoffrey Parrinder (Paul Hamlyn, 1967).

African Textiles by John Picton and John Mack (Harper & Row, 1989).

Arts and Crafts of Mexico by Chloe Sayer (Chronicle Books, 1990).

Children Are Children Are Children by Anne Cole, Carolyn Haas, and Betty Weinberger (Little, Brown, 1978).

Children Around the World by Jane Caballero and Derek Whordley (Humanics, 1983).

Copycats and Artifacts by Marianne Ford (David Godine, 1986).

Folk Arts Around the World and How to Make Each One by Virginie Fowler (Prentice-Hall, 1981).

Hieroglyphs: The Writing of Ancient Egypt by Norma Jean Katan (Atheneum, 1981).

India Celebrates! by Jane Werner Watson (Garrard, 1974).

Inuit Peoples of Canada by Palmer Patterson (Grolier, 1982).

Kwanzaa: An African-American Celebration of Culture and Cooking by Eric Copage (Morrow, 1991).

Meaning in Crafts by Edward L. Mattil (Prentice-Hall, 1971).

Primitive and Folk Jewelry by Michael Haberlandt (Dover, 1971).

The You and Me Heritage Tree Ethnic Crafts for Children by Phyllis and Noel Fiarotta (Workman, 1976).